BRENT LIBRARIES

Please return/renew this item
by the last date shown.
Books may also be renewed by
phone or online.
Tel: 0333 370 4700
On-line www.brent.gov.uk/libraryservice

ELECTRICITY

BY
JOANNA BRUNDLE

©2017
Book Life
King's Lynn
Norfolk PE30 4LS

ISBN: 978-1-78637-207-9

Written by:
Joanna Brundle

Edited by:
Charlie Ogden

Designed by:
Drue Rintoul

A catalogue record for this book
is available from the British Library.

Photocredits
Abbreviations: l-left, r-right, b-bottom, t-top, c-centre, m-middle.

Front Cover t – chuyuss. Front Cover mt – VioNet. Front Cover mb – Innershadows Photography. Front Cover b – Posonskyi Andrey. 1. – Anastasiya Aleksandrenko. 2 – zhengzaishuru. 3b – Dino Osmic. 3t – rangizzz. 4tr – rkl_foto. 4b – studiovin. 5tl – MrJafari. 5b – STILLFX. 6tr – Vladimir Wrangel. 6ml – patrice6000. 6b – In The Light Photography. 7t – HE68. 7b – Guas, johnjohnson, Vasily Kovalev. 8tr – JRP Studio. 8ml – givaga. 8br – Audrius Merfeldas. 9tr – khuruzero. 9br – anaken2012. 9bl – Dino Osmic. 10t – Vaclav Mach. 10b – arogant. 11t – Tony Moran. 11b – KanitChurem. 12tr – haryigit. 12b – Marbury. 13tr – Innershadows Photography. 14tr – rangizzz. 14b – Peshkova. 15l – Lisses. 15br – qwasder1987. 15bl – I. Pilon. 16tl – montree imnam. 18tr – Love Silhouette. 18b – David Papazian. 19t – Jochen Schoenfeld. 19b – yelantsevv. 19bl – Chaay_Tee. 20 – CHAINFOTO24. 21tr – ChiccoDodiFC. 21b – kaband. 22tm – imagedb.com. 22bl – haryigit. 23t – dvande. 23b – r.nagy. 24tr – aoy jira. 24tr – Lisa S. 24b – Andrey_Popov. 25tr – Mrs_ya. 25b – Caron Badkin. 26t – Satyrenko. 26br – Dario Lo Presti. 27r – Gagliardilmages. 27bl – AkeSak. 28c – titoOnz. 29t – Ivica Drusany. 29b – otomobil. 30t – Claudio Divizia. 30b – Vasilius.Images are courtesy of Shutterstock.com. With thanks to Getty Images, Thinkstock Photo and iStockphoto.

CONTENTS

Words that look like **this** are explained in the glossary on page 31.

WHAT IS ELECTRICITY?

Has there ever been a power cut at your home? If there has, then you will know how important electricity is. How did it feel to sit in the dark with no television to watch?

Electricity is a very useful form of energy. It can easily be changed into heat, light, sound or movement energy. It can also flow through **cables**, which makes it easy to move electricity to where it is needed. Electricity powers many devices, from hairdryers to washing machines, and provides heat and light in homes, businesses, schools and hospitals.

In some parts of the world, there is never any electricity available. People have to cook their food on a fire and wash their clothes in a river.

HOW MANY TIMES DO YOU THINK YOU USE ELECTRICITY EACH DAY? TRY KEEPING A RECORD OF EVERY TIME YOU USE IT. REMEMBER TO INCLUDE THINGS THAT ARE POWERED BY BATTERIES. DO THE RESULTS SURPRISE YOU?

All these devices change electrical energy into other forms of energy.

ELECTRIC CHARGE

Everything is made up of tiny **particles** called **atoms**. Inside every atom is a **nucleus**. An atom's nucleus contains even tinier particles called **protons** and **neutrons**. The nucleus is surrounded by a cloud of moving particles called **electrons**.

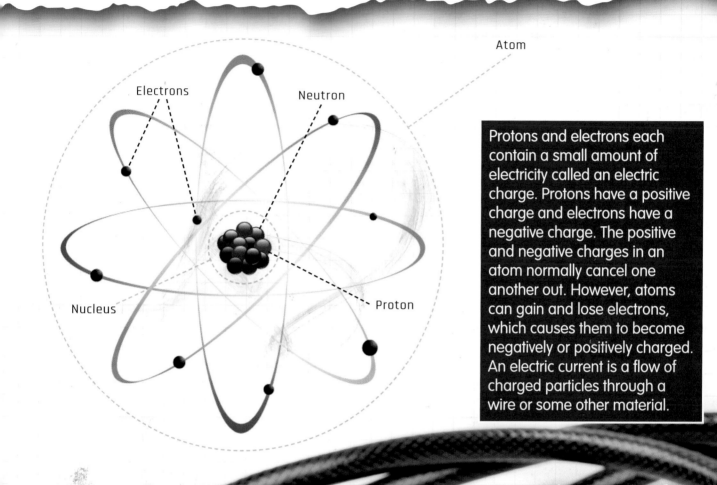

Atom

Electrons

Neutron

Nucleus

Proton

Protons and electrons each contain a small amount of electricity called an electric charge. Protons have a positive charge and electrons have a negative charge. The positive and negative charges in an atom normally cancel one another out. However, atoms can gain and lose electrons, which causes them to become negatively or positively charged. An electric current is a flow of charged particles through a wire or some other material.

The flow of electric current through a wire is like the flow of water through a hosepipe.

NATURAL ELECTRICITY

Many examples of electricity can be seen in the natural world. Electric eels live in rivers in South America. They are able to give the creatures they are hunting an **electric shock**, which makes it easy for the eels to catch and eat them.

Electric Eel

Electrical signals send messages and information around the brains of animals, including humans.

The Human Brain

If you rub a balloon on your head, static electricity can make your hair stand on end!

STATIC ELECTRICITY

Things that do not conduct electricity, meaning that electricity cannot flow through them, are called insulators or insulating materials. An electric charge can build up on the surface of an insulating material. This happens because the electric charge cannot flow through it. This electric charge is called static electricity. By rubbing certain things together, such as a blown-up balloon and a jumper, you can make static electricity. The balloon becomes negatively charged and the jumper becomes positively charged. Opposite charges attract, so the balloon sticks to the jumper.

LIGHTNING

Scientists believe that lightning is caused by static electricity. Inside storm clouds, electric charges build up as water droplets and tiny pieces of ice rub against each other. If enough of a charge builds up, a spark of electrical energy jumps between the cloud and the ground. The electrical energy changes into light energy, which is why we see lightning. It also changes into sound energy, which is why we hear thunder.

The temperature inside a bolt of lightning is around 28,000°**C**. That's five times hotter than the surface of the Sun.

Static electricity can be useful. Spray paint is used to paint fences and parts of cars. As the paint leaves the spray can, the particles all become positively charged. Things that have the same charge repel each other. As all the paint particles are positively charged, they repel, or push away from, one another. This helps the paint to spread evenly over the surface.

CURRENT ELECTRICITY

Current electricity is not the same as static electricity. Static electricity stays on the surface of objects. Current electricity flows as a stream of electrons through a material. But electrons don't flow on their own – they need a push! This push is called an **electromotive force** (EMF). The EMF in many small objects, such as torches and television remotes, comes from their batteries. What other battery-powered objects can you think of?

Mobile phones are battery-powered.

Drone

Remote-Controlled Car

BATTERIES

Batteries are very useful because they are easy to carry around. They can be used to power things that we want to use on the move, such as mobile phones.

DID YOU KNOW? BATTERIES ARE MADE UP OF 'CELLS'. SCIENTISTS USUALLY USE THE WORD 'CELL' INSTEAD OF THE WORD 'BATTERY'. A BATTERY IS MADE UP OF TWO OR MORE CELLS.

8

BATTERY LIFE

Switching on battery-powered objects gradually uses up the battery's stored chemical energy. Eventually, the chemicals are used up and the battery stops giving out a current. When this happens, we say the battery has 'gone flat'. Batteries that cannot then be recharged and have to be thrown away are called primary cells. Secondary cells are batteries that can be recharged and used again. How long a battery lasts – which is known as its battery life – depends on the device being used. Some apps on smartphones, for example, use a lot of battery power, whereas other devices, such as television remotes, use only a little battery power.

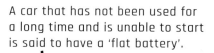

TYPES OF BATTERY

Batteries come in different shapes and sizes and give out different amounts of electric current depending on what they are used for. Car batteries are large and heavy. The electrical energy from a car battery starts the car's engine. As the engine runs, it recharges the battery. Small button batteries are used in watches, calculators, hearing aids and toys.

A car that has not been used for a long time and is unable to start is said to have a 'flat battery'.

Small children should not be allowed near button batteries because they can easily be swallowed. The chemicals they contain can cause serious burns inside the body.

MAINS ELECTRICITY

*Most of us use **mains electricity** to get the energy we need. Special factories called power stations produce mains electricity on a huge scale.*

Power Station

Inside a power station, a fuel, such as coal or natural gas, is burned. As it burns, the fuel gives off heat, which is used to boil water. Steam from the water is used to turn fan-like blades on a machine called a turbine. This allows the turbine to spin magnets that sit inside a coil of wire in a **generator**. This creates an electric current. Some power stations use **nuclear energy** to boil water instead of burning fuel. All power stations that use heat to boil water are called thermal power stations.

Turbine Blades

10

Generators can be powered by many different types of energy. Hydroelectric power stations use the force of fast-flowing water to spin the turbines. At a tidal power station, the force used to spin the turbines comes from the tide coming in and out. Wind turbines have blades that spin in the wind and turn the magnets inside generators.

A group of wind turbines, called a wind farm, can be built on land or out at sea.

THE GRID SYSTEM

Power stations and electricity cables are all joined together. They make a huge network called the national grid. If there is high demand for electricity in an area, or if part of the grid isn't working properly, power can still be sent wherever it is needed. The demand for electricity is usually highest in the evening. Can you think why this is so?

DID YOU KNOW? FOSSIL FUELS, SUCH AS COAL AND OIL, WILL EVENTUALLY RUN OUT IF WE KEEP USING THEM. THEY ARE DESCRIBED AS NON-RENEWABLE BECAUSE THEY CANNOT BE REPLACED. ALTERNATIVE TYPES OF ENERGY, SUCH AS SOLAR POWER AND WIND POWER, ARE DESCRIBED AS RENEWABLE BECAUSE THEY WILL NOT RUN OUT IF WE KEEP USING THEM.

Falling trees or strong winds can bring down power cables and cause power cuts.

CIRCUITS

An electric current can only flow in a complete loop called a circuit. The electrical current that flows through a circuit powers the devices that are part of that circuit, such as a lightbulb. As long as there are no gaps in the circuit, the device will keep working. If the circuit is broken, the device will stop working. Circuits are found in everything that uses electricity, such as cars, televisions, traffic lights and torches.

COMPONENTS

The different parts that make up a circuit are called components. A simple circuit is called a **series circuit**. It includes a power source, wires, a switch and a device, such as a lamp or buzzer.

The components in a series circuit are arranged in a single loop. Each component must be connected to the next one in the circuit, otherwise the circuit will be broken and the device won't work. Each component in a series circuit has a job to do. For example, the bulb gives out light when the current passes through it. The same amount of current passes through each component in the circuit.

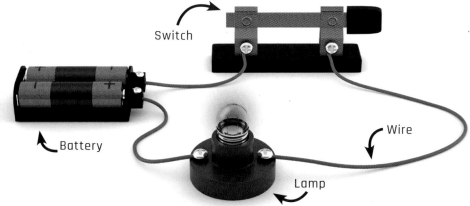

Switch

Battery

Wire

Lamp

The electrical current passes from the battery, through the wire and through each component before returning to the battery.

If any component stops working, the circuit is broken and the device will not work. If one light bulb fails, none of them will work because the circuit is no longer complete.

SWITCHES

Switches start and stop the flow of current in a circuit. When you switch on any electrical device, such as a torch, you complete the circuit and the device works. When you switch it off, the circuit is broken and the device stops working. When you use a wall **socket**, you turn the mains electricity on or off in the same way. When you plug something in and turn on the switch, you complete the circuit. Unplugging something or turning off the switch breaks the circuit.

Wall Sockets

Most wall sockets have a switch. They have to be switched on before an electric current will flow.

ELECTRICAL SYMBOLS

Symbols are signs that we use to represent, or stand for, something else. If you know a symbol, you can recognise and understand it whatever language you speak. Special symbols are used in diagrams to represent the components in electrical circuits. They help people who work with electricity to understand complicated **circuit diagrams**.

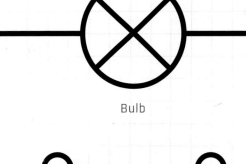

Bulb

Switch (Open)

Switch (Closed)

Wire

Cell

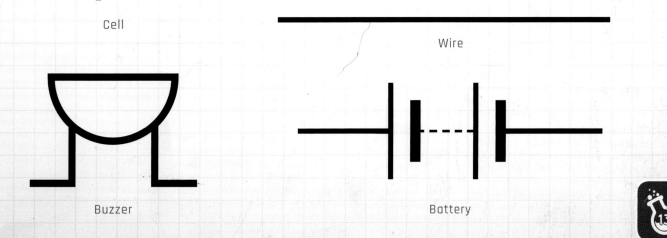

Buzzer

Battery

CHANGING CIRCUITS

Changing the components in a circuit can give different results. When extra batteries are added to a circuit, the devices in the circuit will work harder. Bulbs will shine more brightly and buzzers will ring louder. Taking batteries away will make bulbs less bright and buzzers less loud.

BULBS

If more bulbs are added to a circuit, without adding extra batteries, each bulb will shine less brightly. In a circuit with one battery and two bulbs, for example, each of the two bulbs will shine less brightly than one bulb would shine. However, the two bulbs will also be equally bright. One will not be brighter than the other.

DID YOU KNOW? BATTERIES HAVE TO BE PUT TOGETHER CORRECTLY IN A CIRCUIT, OTHERWISE THE DEVICE THEY ARE POWERING WON'T WORK. A **POSITIVE TERMINAL** MUST ALWAYS BE CONNECTED TO A **NEGATIVE TERMINAL**.

WIRES

It is harder for an electric current to pass through thin wires than it is for an electric current to pass through thick wires. A thin wire is said to have more **resistance** to the flow of electricity. A motor will run more slowly in a circuit that contains thin wires than in a circuit that contains thick wires. Thin wires stop electricity from flowing well. Longer wires will also make a motor run more slowly or a bulb shine less brightly than shorter wires.

DID YOU KNOW? CIRCUIT COMPONENTS THAT ARE HARD FOR AN ELECTRICAL CURRENT TO PASS THROUGH ARE CALLED RESISTORS. THEY ARE USED TO CHANGE THE VOLUME – OR LOUDNESS – OF RADIOS.

ELECTRIC MOTORS

An electric motor can be added to a circuit. Electric motors change electrical energy into movement energy. These components are used in numerous objects, from toy cars to real cars!

Inside a remote-controlled car is a simple electric motor. Inside this motor, electric current from the battery passes through a flat wire coil. The coil is held between two magnets. As the current flows, the coil and the magnets produce a turning force. The part of the motor that turns is connected to the wheels of the toy car to make them move. You can make an electrical motor run faster by adding batteries to the circuit.

MEASURING ELECTRICITY

There are special units of measurement for electricity. They are named after scientists who made important discoveries about electricity.

AMPERES (A)

The amount of electrical current moving through a wire is measured in amperes or amps. Amps are measured using an ammeter.

Ammeter

A current of one amp means that six million, million, million electrons are flowing past a point in the wire every second. A hairdryer uses around ten amps, but a phone charger uses less than 0.5 amps. The amp is named after the French scientist André -Marie Ampère (1775-1836).

VOLTS (V)

The electromotive force (see page 8) that pushes an electrical current is measured in volts, using a voltmeter. A torch battery produces about one and a half volts, whereas cables carried on **pylons** have an EMF of up to 400,000 volts. The volt is named after the Italian scientist Alessandro Volta (1745-1827).

The first battery, called the voltaic pile, was invented by Volta in 1799. It was made of zinc and copper discs, separated by pieces of cloth soaked in salt water.

OHMS (Ω)

Resistors try to slow down the electrical current flowing through them. This is called electrical resistance. The wire inside an old-fashioned light bulb is a resistor. It slows down the current, which makes the wire get very hot and glow brightly. Electrical resistance is measured in ohms. The ohm is named after the German scientist Georg Ohm (1789-1854).

Georg Ohm

WATTS (W)

The amount of electrical energy that something uses in a second is measured in watts. A kilowatt is the word used for 1,000 watts. A smartphone charger uses about seven watts, but an air conditioning unit can use up to 4,000 watts, or four kilowatts. The watt is named after the Scottish engineer James Watt (1736-1819).

James Watt

CONDUCTORS AND INSULATORS

Electrical conductors are materials that allow electricity to pass through them. Metals are very good electrical conductors. Electrical wires and cables are made of metal so that electricity can pass through them easily. Most non-metals are poor conductors of electricity.

GOOD AND BAD CONDUCTORS

Copper, aluminium, iron and **steel** are all excellent electrical conductors.

Graphite is a material found in pencils. It is an unusual material because it is a non-metal that conducts electricity well. Water is also a non-metal that can conduct electricity. We have to keep electrical equipment away from water so that we don't get an electric shock.

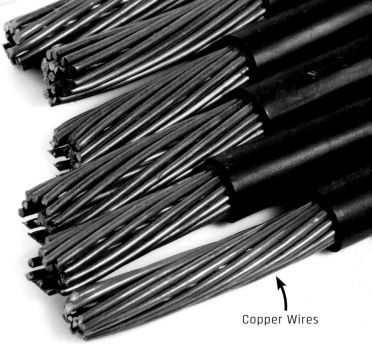

Copper Wires

Lights in a bathroom are turned on using a cord pull or a switch outside the bathroom. This is because using an ordinary wall switch with wet hands could give you an electric shock.

18

INSULATORS

Materials that electricity cannot flow through are called insulators. Plastic, glass, rubber and wood are all good insulators, meaning that they do not conduct electricity. Insulators are used to stop electricity from flowing where it is not wanted. In copper cables, for example, the plastic that covers the cables stops the current from escaping and allows it to reach the device that it is powering.

Around the world, plugs have different shapes and may have two or three pins. The metal pins conduct electricity. The plastic or rubber casing is an insulator that makes the plug safe to hold.

PYLONS

Pylons are made of metal, so you might expect that they would conduct electricity from the cables they carry. This would be rather dangerous! Luckily, insulators made of glass or porcelain (a type of china) make sure the cables don't touch the metal pylons and that the electricity remains safely in the cables.

Pylon

Porcelain Insulators

ELECTRICITY'S JOURNEY

Power stations feed electricity into the grid system. Before the electricity can begin its journey, its voltage (the pushing force that makes the current flow) has to be changed. Devices called step-up transformers are used to do this. They increase the voltage from about 22,000 volts to about 400,000 volts. The electricity then begins its journey through thick cables. The high voltage electricity in these cables is extremely dangerous, which is why the cables are held up by tall pylons. At this stage, the electricity's voltage is too high for it to be used.

When electricity cables need to be repaired, special lifting equipment is used so that workers can reach them. The current must be switched off before work begins.

SOME PEOPLE THINK THAT PYLONS SPOIL THE COUNTRYSIDE. WHAT DO YOU THINK? IT IS MUCH MORE EXPENSIVE TO LAY CABLES UNDERGROUND THAN TO USE PYLONS.

SUB-STATIONS

Electricity sub-stations are places where the voltage is reduced to a level that is useful. This is done by different transformers, called step-down transformers. Sub-stations are found close to where electricity is needed. Underground cables carry the electricity the rest of the way into our homes, businesses, schools and hospitals.

Different places need electricity of different voltages. Some factories, such as those that make steel, need electricity at 33,000 volts. Houses usually need electricity at 110 or 240 volts.

Electric cables being laid underground.

Overhead cables supply power to high-speed electric trains. Sub-stations are often found close to railway tracks.

ELECTRICITY AND MAGNETISM

Magnetism is an invisible force that attracts (pulls towards) or repels (pushes away) some materials. A magnetic field is the area around a magnet where its magnetism can be felt. Magnetic materials are ones that are attracted to magnets or ones that can become magnets. Very few materials are magnetic. The most common magnetic material is iron. Steel is also magnetic because it contains a lot of iron.

Iron filings scattered around a magnet move to show its magnetic field.

ELECTROMAGNET

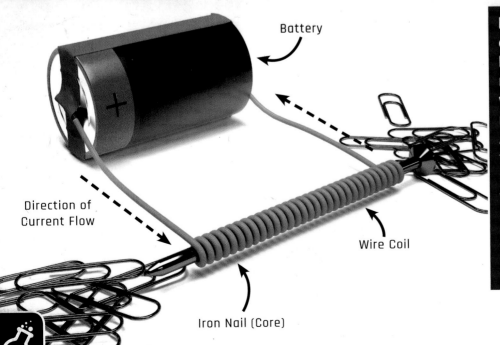

Battery

Direction of Current Flow

Wire Coil

Iron Nail (Core)

Electricity and magnetism are very closely linked. Electromagnetism is the name of the force produced when electricity and magnetism work together. An electrical current passing through a wire creates a magnetic field around the wire. If the wire is coiled around a metal **core**, the core becomes magnetised too – and an electromagnet has been made.

USING ELECTROMAGNETS

Electromagnets are very useful. Powerful electromagnets are used for lifting heavy loads of metal. On a building site, for example, they can be used to move steel from one place to another. When the steel has been moved, the current can be switched off. When the current is switched off, the magnetism is lost. The load then drops down wherever it is needed.

A powerful electromagnet is being used at this junkyard to separate valuable iron and steel from rubbish.

MAGLEV TRAINS

A magnet floating in water will always point in a north-south direction. A magnet has a north-seeking and a south-seeking **pole**. Opposite poles (i.e. a north pole and a south pole) attract but the same poles (i.e. a north pole and a north pole) repel or push away. Magnetic levitation trains – or Maglev trains, as they are commonly called – have electromagnets underneath them and run on electromagnetic tracks. The two sets of magnets are arranged so that they repel one another. The train therefore sits just above the track.

Because there is very little **friction** between the train and the track, maglev trains move quickly and smoothly and use less energy than other trains.

23

ELECTRICITY AT HOME

The cables that bring electricity into our homes lead to a meter. A meter measures how much electricity we use. Electricity companies use the information from the meter to work out how much electricity we have used and how much we need to pay them. Do you know where your electricity meter is at home? Ask whoever you live with to show you where it is. You can see the numbers changing as electricity is used.

The cable then goes to a box called a **consumer unit**. From here, it connects to the different circuits that allow us to use electricity all around the house. Cookers, as well as other equipment like refrigerators, wall sockets and lighting, all have their own circuits.

Electricity Meter

Using separate circuits around the house allows us to switch off the power to the oven while still having the kitchen lights on.

FUSES

A consumer unit is sometimes called a fuse box. Each circuit has a fuse or a device called a **circuit breaker** in the consumer unit. If there is a problem with the circuit or with something plugged into the circuit, the fuse or circuit breaker switches off the current to keep us safe. Fuses have to be replaced afterwards. Circuit breakers can simply be reset.

A fuse contains a piece of wire between two screws. If the current becomes too great, the wire gets hot, melts and breaks the circuit.

Plugs contain a fuse that 'blows' and breaks the circuit if there is a problem with the current or with the equipment that is plugged in.

ELECTRICITY IN HOSPITALS

Nerves connect our brains to the other parts of our bodies. Nerves are like message motorways, sending messages between the body and the brain. All this information travels as nerve signals, which are tiny pulses of electrical energy. Doctors can use special machines to pick up and monitor these nerve signals. This helps them to find out what is wrong with patients. An EMG machine measures electrical signals in a patient's muscles. This tells the doctor if there is muscle weakness or if a patient is paralysed.

This patient is having an ECG (Electrocardiograph) test. The ECG machine measures electrical signals in the heart to check if it is working properly.

If a patient has a heart attack, their heart may stop beating. A defibrillator is a life-saving machine that sends a pulse of electricity through a patient's body to shock the heart back into beating normally again.

Defibrillator

A defibrillator has two metal plates that are placed on a patient's body. The plates have plastic handles that act as insulators so that only the patient receives an electric shock.

ELECTROMAGNETS IN HOSPITALS

Electromagnets are useful in hospitals. They are used to remove small pieces of metal from the bodies of patients who have been hurt, for example in a car accident.

The surgeon can increase the electrical current until the magnet has just enough power to pull and gently remove the unwanted metal.

MRI SCANNERS

An MRI scanner is a large tube surrounded by a giant circular electromagnet. The patient lays on a special bed that can be moved in and out of the scanner. MRI scanners create a magnetic field around the patient's body. They look at the way a patient's body reacts to this magnetic field. This information is used to form pictures of the inside of the patient's body.

MRI Scanner

MRI Brain Scan

An MRI scan gives a doctor a clear picture of what is happening inside the patient's body, without the need for an operation.

ELECTRICITY AND THE ENVIRONMENT

Have you ever wondered why people are always asking you to turn off lights and other electrical equipment that you're not using? It's partly because electricity is expensive to use. But there is another very important reason.

GLOBAL WARMING

Most of the electricity that we use still comes from power stations that burn fossil fuels like coal and natural gas. Burning fossil fuels releases **carbon dioxide** into the air. Carbon dioxide is a **greenhouse gas**. Greenhouse gases trap heat in the atmosphere around the Earth, which is slowly causing temperatures on Earth to rise. This effect is called global warming.

CLIMATE CHANGE

The typical weather for a place is called its climate. In desert areas, for example, the climate is hot and dry with little rain. Although climates do change naturally over hundreds of years, scientists believe that global warming is speeding up this process. Global warming could cause sea levels to rise by melting **polar ice caps**. Flooding could damage homes, crops and **habitats**. If many crops were destroyed, it could also quickly lead to mass starvation and death.

SAVING ELECTRICITY

Everyone can help to slow down global warming by using less electricity. A lower demand for electricity would mean that less fossil fuels would need to be burned and less greenhouse gases would be produced.

Small renewable energy systems that use the power of the Sun (solar energy) or the wind (wind energy) can be fitted to homes.

Wind Turbine

Solar Panel

ELECTRIC CARS - GOOD OR BAD?

Electric cars use rechargeable batteries as a power source. They don't burn fossil fuels and so they don't release carbon dioxide into the atmosphere. But where does the electricity that is used to recharge the batteries come from? It may have been produced in a power station by burning fossil fuels, rather than in one that uses renewable types of energy.

Electric car charging stations are now common in towns and cities all over the world.

STAYING SAFE

ELECTRICITY IS DANGEROUS!

Never climb or go near a pylon or sub-station. You could be electrocuted. Look out for warning signs like this.

DANGER OF DEATH

Never put your fingers into an electrical socket or an electrical appliance such as a toaster. Ask your parents to fit socket covers to protect young children.

STEPPING ON ELECTRIFIED RAILWAY TRACKS CAN KILL YOU INSTANTLY. STAY AWAY!

Don't play outside in a thunderstorm. You could be struck by lightning.

Always make sure that your hands are dry before using any electrical equipment. If you use an electrical device with wet hands, the water can pass the electricity through you. This can hurt or even kill you.

If you see a bare wire poking through plastic casing, tell an adult straightaway. Touching the wire while the appliance is plugged in could give you an electric shock.

GLOSSARY

°C	the symbol for degrees Celsius, the metric measurement of temperature
atoms	the smallest possible particles that something is made of
cables	thick wires
carbon dioxide	a gas that occurs naturally in the atmosphere
circuit breaker	a device that automatically stops the flow of electric current for safety reasons
circuit diagrams	drawings of electrical circuits that use electrical symbols
consumer unit	a device containing a row of fuses or small circuit breakers that controls and distributes electricity
core	the middle or central part of something
electric shock	a sudden flow of electricity through the body that causes pain or death
electromotive force	the pushing force needed to make an electric current flow
electrons	particles in an atom that have a negative charge
fossil fuels	natural energy sources formed over millions of years from the remains of dead animals and plants
friction	a force that tries to stop two materials passing over one another
generator	a device that turns movement energy into electrical current
greenhouse gas	a gas in the Earth's atmosphere that traps heat from the Sun
habitats	the natural homes or environments of plants and animals
mains electricity	electricity that is supplied using the grid system
negative terminal	the flat end of a battery that carries a negative charge
neutrons	particles in an atom that have no electric charge
nuclear energy	energy obtained from the splitting of atoms
nucleus	the centre of an atom
particles	very small pieces of matter
polar ice caps	large areas of ice at the North or South Pole
pole	either of the two ends of a magnet where the pulling and pushing forces are strongest
positive terminal	the knobbly end of a battery that carries a positive charge
protons	particles in an atom that have a positive charge
pylons	tall, metal towers that hold dangerous electrical cables high in the air
resistance	the ability of something to reduce the flow of electric current
series circuit	a single electrical loop in which current passes through the components one after another
socket	a device fitted to a wall to hold a plug and complete an electrical circuit
solar power	energy obtained from the Sun
steel	a strong metal that is made of iron and other substances

INDEX